HSE
Health & Safety
Executive

CW00546162

HM Railway Inspectorate

RAILWAY ACCIDENT AT BEXLEY

A report on the investigation into
the derailment of a freight train at
Bexley on the Dartford Loop line of
Railtrack Southern Zone
on 4 February 1997

HSE BOOKS

© Crown copyright 1999
Applications for reproduction should be made in writing to:
Copyright Unit, Her Majesty's Stationery Office,
St Clements House, 2-16 Colegate, Norwich NR3 1BQ

First published 1999

ISBN 0 7176 1658 4

All rights reserved. No part of this publication may be
reproduced, stored in a retrieval system, or transmitted
in any form or by any means (electronic, mechanical,
photocopying, recording or otherwise) without the prior
written permission of the copyright owner.

CONTENTS

FURTHER ACTION   33

APPENDICES   34

SUMMARY

The Incident

1.   At about 12:11 on Tuesday 4th February 1997 a freight train carrying spoil from railway track renewal work derailed just after passing through Bexley Station, Kent. The train was travelling from Three Bridges, Sussex to Hoo Junction, near Gravesend in Kent, and derailed on Bridge 799 immediately east of Bexley Station as a result of lateral movement of the track on the longitudinal timbers on the bridge and a resultant widening of the track gauge. The two locomotives and the first 11 wagons remained on the track. The 12th wagon remained connected to the eleventh wagon with the rear nearside wheel of the rear wheelset derailed. The train separated to the rear of the 12th wagon. The remaining 7 wagons were completely derailed. This had resulted in substantial damage to the viaduct carrying the track. Four members of the public who were working in or near the arches under the viaduct were injured, and extensive damage was caused to the viaduct and nearby buildings.

The cause

2.   The primary cause of the derailment was spreading of the track gauge on the longitudinal wheeltimbers on Bridge 799, where significant deterioration of the track support and its fastenings had occurred.

3.   Two other factors contributed to the primary cause of the accident. The 12th wagon in the train was overloaded. It derailed but remained upright. This resulted in the forces exerted on the track being on average larger than normal. The train was travelling in excess of the speed limit specified for freight trains on the route. This made a minimal contribution to the accident.

4.   The underlying causes of the derailment were:

  a.   The failure of South East Infrastructure Maintenance Company Ltd (SEIMCL) to manage their organisation. SEIMCL did not have adequate systems or procedures and failed to provide sufficient resources to meet their commitments to ensure that the whole of the railway infrastructure in the eastern part of the Southern Zone was safely maintained. The longitudinal wheeltimbers on Bridge 799 were rotten and had been identified as requiring urgent repairs by SEIMCL. The company did not arrange for any repairs to be undertaken and the track continued to deteriorate until it eventually became unsafe.

  b.   Southern Track Renewals Company Ltd (STRCL) failed to make adequate arrangements to ensure the wagons were in a safely loaded condition.

  c.   Railtrack have ultimate responsibility for ensuring that the railway infrastructure is maintained in a safe condition. They failed to monitor the performance of their contractor (South East Infrastructure Maintenance Company Ltd). The unsafe condition of the track was known of by Railtrack, but they took no action to address this.

d.   The driver of the train had not been adequately trained by Connex South Central (CSC) to operate freight trains.

e.   The arrangements for the inspection, maintenance and calibration of the locomotive speedometers were inadequate.

Recovery and reinstatement

5.   The injured received treatment on site from the emergency services and were treated in hospital.

6.   The two locomotives and 12 wagons were moved to Hoo Junction at reduced speed following rerailing of the 12th wagon on Saturday 8th February. The 13th wagon was removed from the track and left adjacent to the down line. The remaining 6 wagons were removed over some time as the clear up operation progressed.

7.   The viaduct and river bridge were rebuilt. The down line track was reinstated and the line reopened to normal traffic 28 days after the accident.

Investigations

8.   Inspectors from the Health and Safety Executive's Railway Inspectorate attended site on the day of the incident. The investigation commenced that day, and proceeded over several months.

9.   Railtrack undertook their own investigations into the cause of the accident. They employed the services of BR Research (BRR), part of AEA Technology to assist them in the technical aspects of the investigations. The Railtrack investigation was chaired independently and the panel members were from English, Welsh and Scottish Railways, Railtrack Zone and HQ and BRR. There were a number of observers from the other parties involved in the accident.

Lessons to be learnt from the accident

10. This report concludes that a number of lessons should be learnt from the events that led to this accident. These lessons are aimed at preventing a recurrence.

11. Railtrack, train operators, maintainers of the railway infrastructure and owners of the railway rolling stock should look at the lessons to be learnt in this report and consider how they can be put into practice in order to reduce the possibility of an accident resulting from inadequately maintained track happening again. Inspectors from Her Majesty's Railway Inspectorate (HMRI) will monitor how this is done.

Legal proceedings

12. At Kingston Crown Court on 8 September 1998 Railtrack plc, SEIMCL and STRCL were each convicted of offences under the Health & Safety at Work etc. Act 1974 Section 3. The offences were in each case that they failed to ensure the safety of

members of the public, so far as is reasonably practicable.   Fines totalling £150,000:00 were imposed by the judge and two presiding magistrates with costs of £41,768:00 awarded to HSE.

BACKGROUND

The companies involved

13. Railtrack plc is the Infrastructure Controller of the national railway network and operator of a number of designated major stations. This includes approximately 23,000 track miles, 2,482 stations and 90,000 bridges Railtrack was formed on 1st April 1994 as part of the privatisation of the railway network. Approximately 11,650 people were employed by Railtrack at the time of the incident.

14. The whole infrastructure of track, signalling and electrification at the accident location is owned by Railtrack plc. On a local basis this is managed by the Southern Zone of Railtrack

15. The maintenance of the whole of the infrastructure of track, signalling and electrification in the eastern part of the Southern Zone in Kent, including the accident site, is done under contract to Railtrack by South East Infrastructure Maintenance Company Limited (SEIMCL) which is a subsidiary of Balfour Beatty Rail Limited.

16. The renewal of the track within the Southern Zone is done under contract to Railtrack by Southern Track Renewals Company Limited (STRCL) which is another subsidiary of Balfour Beatty Rail Limited.

17. The operation of freight trains to facilitate both the maintenance and renewal of the infrastructure is carried out under contract to Railtrack by English, Welsh and Scottish Railways, a company owned by Wisconsin Central Transportation Ltd. Both SEIMCL and STRCL are parties to this contract. The wagon that initiated the derailment and was overloaded belonged to CAIB UK Limited. The remaining wagons in the train are owned either by CAIB UK Limited or Tiphook Rail Limited and leased to the user.

18. The freight train was driven by a Connex South Central (CSC) driver. CSC are contracted by EWS to provide train crew for freight trains as required.

19. A fundamental part of the investigation was to establish the interaction of these companies and how they worked together to ensure safe train operation and infrastructure integrity.

Location of the accident

20. The accident occurred where the railway from Lee to Crayford passes through Bexley. A site location diagram is shown in figure 1. The railway through Bexley station is part of the line known as the Dartford Loop and is used mainly by suburban passenger trains, with some freight traffic. East of the station it crosses Old Bexley High Street on a steel decked bridge, which is numbered 799. This bridge runs on to a brick built viaduct about eight metres high, typical of many locations in built up areas. The arches of the viaduct were at the time of the accident occupied by various businesses including garages and workshops. There are two lines of track running from Lee to Crayford designated from north to south as the down line (trains travelling away from

London) and the up line (trains travelling towards London). The train; 6Y56 was travelling east on the down line and had just passed through Bexley Station when it derailed on Bridge 799.

21.   The down line through Bexley Station is on a slight left hand curve; as the track passes over bridge 799 it is nominally straight and then curves to the right. The down line was supported on concrete sleepers prior to Bridge 799, longitudinal wheeltimbers over the bridge, wooden sleepers over the viaduct and concrete sleepers after that. Sleepers are positioned at right angles to the track and support both rails and hold them to the correct gauge using chairs and chair screws. Sleepers are made of concrete, wood or steel depending on the location in which they are to be used. However, on bridge 799 the rails are supported on longitudinal wheeltimbers which run parallel to the track under each rail. The bridge structure locates the wheeltimbers in position and holds the rails to gauge using baseplates and chair screws.

22.   Trains are controlled in this area by signalling operated from Dartford Signalling Centre. The signals are 4-aspect colour light signals with associated Automatic Warning System. All lines are track circuited, signalling being by the Track Circuit Block method. The maximum train speed permitted on this line was 60 mph, but the maximum permitted speed for freight trains was 40 mph.

23.   The railway in this area is electrified on the third rail direct current system and energised at 750 volts. The system in the area is supervised from an electrical control room at Lewisham.

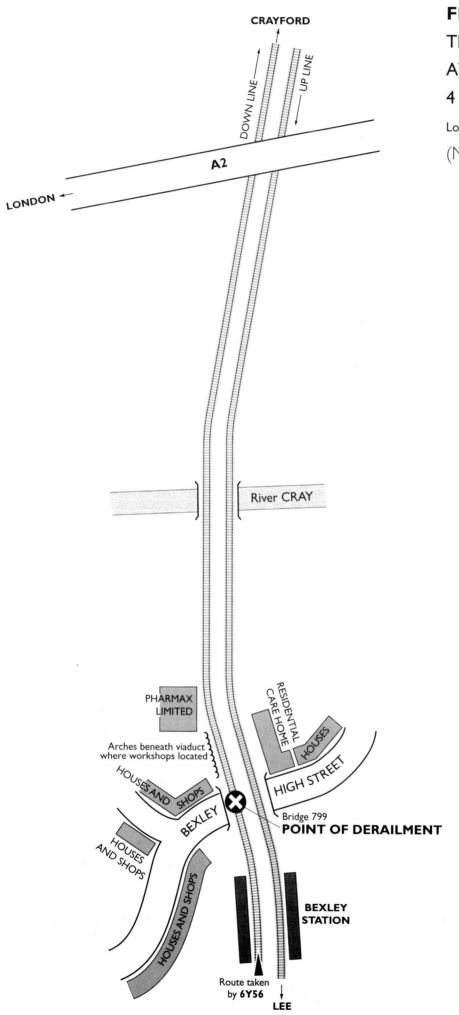

TRAIN DERAILMENT
AT BEXLEY,
4 FEBRUARY 1997

Location plan

(NOT TO SCALE)

CRAYFORD

DOWN LINE

UP LINE

A2

LONDON

River CRAY

PHARMAX
LIMITED

RESIDENTIAL
CARE HOME

HOUSES

Arches beneath viaduct
where workshops located

HOUSES AND SHOPS

HIGH STREET

BEXLEY

Bridge 799
POINT OF DERAILMENT

HOUSES
AND SHOPS

HOUSES AND SHOPS

**BEXLEY
STATION**

Route taken
by **6Y56**

LEE

THE ACCIDENT

The train

24. The train that derailed at Bridge 799, Bexley was a freight train, reporting number 6Y56. The formation of the train when the accident occurred is listed in detail in Appendix 1.

25. The train was operated by English, Welsh and Scottish Railways Ltd. a company owned by Wisconsin Central Transportation Ltd. The wagons on the train had been brought to the yard at Three Bridges, Sussex, from a track renewals site between Billingshurst and Pulborough, West Sussex, where a number of them had been loaded with spoil (dirty ballast) by Southern Track Renewals Company Limited (STRCL). The train consisted of 19 wagons. Three of these wagons were empty, eight were partially loaded and eight were fully loaded. The train was due to travel from Three Bridges yard to Hoo Junction, near Gravesend in Kent, for unloading. It travelled via East Croydon, Crystal Palace, Clapham Junction, Lewisham and Hither Green to Bexley, and should have continued on through Dartford to Hoo Junction.

26. The train left Three Bridges at 10:18 hours on Tuesday 4th February after having been routinely examined by an EWS Shunter the previous evening. The loaded wagons had been examined by a Wagon Examiner on arrival at Three Bridges depot on the previous Sunday. The train was hauled by two class 37 diesel locomotives numbers 37167 and 37220. The train was driven from the leading locomotive number (37167) by a driver from Connex South Central's Norwood depot. The driver was accompanied by a relief driver (trainman) from Connex South Central's Redhill depot.

Events prior to the derailment

27. The train proceeded normally from Three Bridges to Nunhead. The leading loco shut down at Nunhead, but the driver managed to restart it without any difficulty. The train continued its journey to Hoo Junction. As the train approached Bexley Station it was travelling between 51 - 59 mph. This was more than the maximum permitted speed for freight trains on the route which was 40 mph.

28. After passing through Bexley Station the driver described feeling "a small snatch followed by a larger snatch". The brakes automatically applied. The trainman looked back out of the window and "saw dust billowing out from the rear of the train".

Immediate consequences and actions of those involved

29. When the train stopped, the driver and trainman inspected it and realised it was incomplete. The trainman placed track circuit operating clips and detonators on the adjacent up line and obtained the signaller's assurance that the line was protected.

30. The driver and trainman then walked back, about 1/3 mile, towards Bexley Station to locate the rear portion of the train. As they walked they heard sirens which suggested a more serious incident than a divided train.

Description of accident site

31.   The accident site is shown in figure 2 and in photographs 1 to 9. The train ended up split into three sections. The first eleven wagons and two locomotives did not derail. The 12th wagon rear nearside wheel (in the direction of travel) derailed into the space between the rails (the "four foot"), and the wheel was found to have moved in on the axle (see paras. 44 and 89 to 93). The 13th wagon came to rest approximately 422m (21 chains or 462 yards) behind the 12th wagon. The bogies and wagon body separated and came to rest adjacent to the down line with one of the bogies in a river that runs below the railway. The other bogie remained on the track. The load from the 13th wagon was scattered as it derailed. The river bridge suffered damage to its parapet wall and the arch. The rear six wagons which were loaded with spoil veered to the left as they derailed at Bridge 799 and landed in the area below the viaduct. Several of the wagon bodies, bogies, wheels and wheelsets separated. A large amount of the load from the wagons, had spilt. On three of the wheelsets from wagons 14 to 18 the cess side wheel (left hand side in the direction of travel) had moved on its axle.

32.   The damage to the viaduct was substantial. A number of brickwork arch rings and the parapet walls were completely destroyed. The area below the viaduct was a working area for the people with businesses located in the arches beneath the viaduct; such as motor vehicle repairers, and a car park for Pharmax Limited, a chemical firm. The 14th wagon came to rest against the Pharmax building and caused minor damage to the fabric of the building.

33.   The track had been completely destroyed from Bridge 799 for a distance of 261 m (286 yards). For a further distance of 422 m (462 yards) the left hand (cess side) rail had been prised from its housings destroying the sleepers, fastenings and rail clips in the process. Photographs 1 to 9 show the accident location and damage caused.

Casualties

34.   The wagons partially demolished the viaduct as it derailed and large amounts of spoil cascaded into the area below. There were members of the public either in or adjacent to the arches of the viaduct when the train derailed. Four of these people were seriously injured. They suffered cuts, bruises and shock. It is fortunate that no-one was killed.

Control of the accident site and ensuing investigation

35.   The emergency services that responded to the incident included; the Metropolitan Police, British Transport Police, London Ambulance Service and London Fire Brigade. All the emergency services worked well together to ensure the effective management of the site in the immediate aftermath of the derailment.

36.   The accident site was declared a crime scene by BTP immediately following the derailment,. This was because of the possibility of there being a fatality/fatalities as a consequence of the accident. Once it had been established that there were no bodies under the rubble the site was released.

37.　Four members of the public were seriously injured as a result of the accident. They were admitted to Queen Mary's Hospital, Sidcup to receive treatment following the accident.

38.　The large number of representatives people and of different companies and organisations at the scene made it extremely difficult to establish who had a legitimate right of access. For this reason and in the interests of preserving evidence the area around the point of derailment was cordoned off by BTP to ensure preservation of the evidence and to assist HMRI in carrying out its investigation. Access was prohibited without specific authorisation. Access was permitted to those persons/companies who demonstrated a legitimate reason for being there. Prior to the destruction of any of the site evidence, which included the removal of the longitudinal wheeltimbers, damaged wheelsets, overloaded wagon etc. all persons/companies were offered the opportunity to inspect the evidence. The tests on both the wheelsets and the longitudinal wheeltimbers were open to monitoring/input by persons/companies with a legitimate interest.

39.　An inter agency debriefing was subsequently held and attended by the investigating HMRI Inspector. The purpose of this review was to examine systems, equipment and resources deployed with a view to identifying any areas for improvement

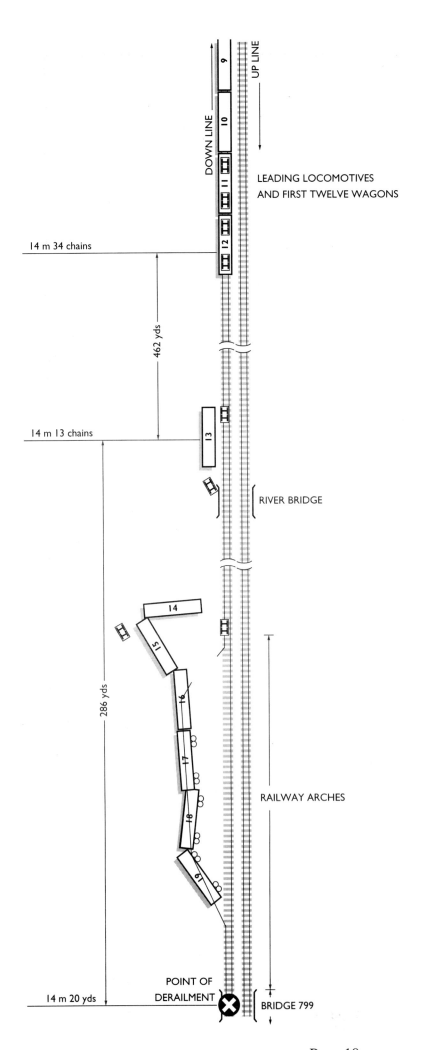

FIGURE 2:
TRAIN DERAILMENT AT BEXLEY, 4 FEBRUARY 1997

Showing relative positions of wagons after accident.

Wagons 1-8 and the two leading locomotives are not shown

(NOT TO SCALE)

PHOTOGRAPH 1
Accident looking from Lee towards Crayford.
The train was travelling from the bottom to the top of the photograph.

HSE INVESTIGATION OF THE ACCIDENT

Background

40.	HM Railway Inspectorate (HMRI) were made aware of the accident at approximately 12:30 hours on 4 February 1997 and contacted Railtrack to obtain further information. An inspector arrived on site at approximately 15:00 hours. The Metropolitan Police, British Transport Police (BTP), London Ambulance Service and London Fire Service, were already in attendance. The Metropolitan Police in conjunction with British Transport Police were maintaining a cordon around the site to prevent unauthorised access. Initial site examinations were therefore carried out jointly by officers from, BTP and HMRI. Some witness statements were taken by BTP and these were made freely available to HMRI.

41.	Railtrack had called in a specialist derailment investigation team from BR Research (BRR), Derby, to carry out a thorough investigation as to the immediate cause of the accident. Their report into the cause of the derailment was made available to HMRI. HMRI worked alongside the BRR team and were satisfied as to the quality and probity of their work. Railtrack also made their own inquiry report available to HMRI in accordance with the Railway Group Standards and mandated by Railtrack's Railway Safety Case.

The direct cause of the accident

42.	A point of derailment was located on the down line 5 baseplates from the east end of the longitudinal wheeltimber at approximately 14 miles 20 yards and about 723 yards from the point where the rear of the twelfth wagon came to a stand. The damage to the track was examined in detail from a point 15 sleepers prior to the point of derailment to the rear of the 19th wagon.

43.	The baseplates and sleepers were numbered for ease of identification from the point of derailment. The point of derailment was designated as point 0, baseplates or sleepers prior to the point of derailment are numbered positively and those after the point of derailment are numbered negatively. Marks on the rail head showed a series of drop-in marks between points 2 and -1 on the cess side (left hand side in the direction of travel), where the wheel had dropped off the rail head into the space between the two running rails (known as the "four foot"). The "six foot" side wheel (right hand side in the direction of travel) had dropped in between the rails from point -11 onwards.

44.	The trailing nearside wheel of the twelfth wagon had derailed and the wheel had moved inwards on its axle. Examination of the track between Sidcup and Bexley produced no evidence to show that the wheel had moved on its axle prior to the derailment. This indicated that the wheel had probably moved on its axle as a result of the derailment and not before.

45.	The 12th wagon PR 3001 was visually assessed as being 80% full. An in-situ assessment of the gross weight of the wagon was made by BRR using specialist equipment. The weight was approximately 120 tonnes.

46.   The overloading of one or more of the wagons in the train imposed forces on the track in excess of those imposed by a "normally loaded" wagon.. This resulted in the gauge spreading forces on the longitudinal wheeltimbers increasing significantly. These gauge spreading forces generated by the axle loads pushed the rails outwards on this already inadequately maintained track sufficiently for the 12th wagon to fall between the rails.

47.   The train was travelling in excess of the permitted line speed. This excess speed imposed additional dynamic forces on the track. There is insufficient knowledge or information available for experts in this narrow field to agree whether the contribution made to the gauge spreading forces by these additional dynamic forces were significant. HSE is therefore unable to determine the relative risk arising from this factor.

48.   The accident at Bexley on Tuesday 4th February 1997 was caused by the track gauge spreading on Bridge 799. The track was supported on longitudinal wheeltimbers over this bridge. There was evidence of significant deterioration of the longitudinal wheeltimbers and their fastenings which allowed the rail chairs and rail to move laterally under load. This is supported by the "drop in" marks on the rail head which confirm that the train derailed on Bridge 799. This is consistent with the HSTRC records showing wide gauge of up to 30 mm in the vicinity.

The signalling equipment

49.   Following an initial assessment of the accident scene it was concluded that the operation of the signalling equipment had no bearing on the cause or consequences of the accident. No further investigation was therefore carried out.

The mechanism of derailment

50.   The initiating event was the derailment of the trailing cess side wheel on wagon PR 3001; the 12th wagon in the train. At the point of derailment, this wheel dropped into the "four foot" and then pushed the left hand rail outwards . The last 7 wagons in the train then also dropped in between the rails from sleeper -11 onwards. The derailed wheel on the twelfth wagon caused substantial damage to the sleepers and the rail fastenings from the bridge over the River Cray at 14 miles 13 chains until it came to rest 422 m (462 yards) further on at 14 miles 34 chains. Wagon PR 3002, the 13th wagon, completely destroyed the track for a distance of 261 m (286 yards) from the point of derailment at approximately 14 miles to the river bridge at 14 miles 13 chains at which point it came to rest with the two bogies separated from the wagon body. The 14th to 19th wagons derailed towards the left hand side in the direction of travel. The 14th wagon turned through 90° as it fell from the viaduct and came to rest against the Pharmax building causing some damage The remaining 5 wagons fell off the viaduct spilling their loads as they fell with little forward momentum. They dropped approximately 8 metres.

The condition of the vehicles

51.	The wagons from the train were examined at the accident site although the rear seven were too badly damaged to enable a full examination to be carried out. The twelfth wagon was found to have the tare weight incorrectly indicated on the side of the vehicle, but this had no bearing on the accident.

52.	The investigation found that the wagon, which was also the first to derail, was substantially overloaded. The gross weight of the wagon was 121.32 tonnes. The permitted gross weight of the wagon is 102 tonnes. Taking into account the tare weight of the wagon of 33 tonnes, this represents an overloading of 28% or 19 tonnes. It was not possible to measure the loads carried by the seven wagons which overturned, but from the volume of spoil that spilled from these wagons the load they carried was also substantial.

53.	No defects were found on the locomotives or the first eleven wagons that could have contributed to the derailment.

The condition of the track

54.	The BRR derailment investigation team carried out a detailed survey of the track on both sides of the point of derailment.

55.	The longitudinal wheeltimbers were constructed in three separate rectangular sections, the central section being smaller than the outer two. The wheeltimbers were sitting within steel troughs. This method of construction relies on the timbers being securely fixed within the troughs by the use of wedges and bitumen or similar Longitudinally along the length of the bridge the wheeltimbers were made up of two lengths. They were not fixed in these troughs. The gap between the timber and the trough was filled with detritus. There was no evidence of wedges to hold the timbers in place. There was some bitumen in the base of the troughs, but this had minimal effect.

56.	Both the tracks over Bridge 799 were completely supported on longitudinal wheeltimbers. The wheeltimbers supporting the down line (the right hand side in the direction of travel) were in a very poor state of repair at the east end of the bridge. The baseplates had sunk into the top surface of the timbers by up to 30 mm. These indentations were up to 20 mm wider than the baseplate in plan. Some of the fixing screws were loose and the timber was split. At several locations there were gaps of up to 20 mm between the base of the baseplates and the top surface of the longitudinal wheeltimbers. These gaps were sufficient to allow the investigating team to put their hands between the underside of the baseplate and the top surface of the wheeltimber

57.	As part of the site investigation the rails were removed from the wheel timbers and the baseplates and their fixings were examined. In some cases the chair screws had rusted to the chairs. The chair screws were not effectively holding the baseplates in place. It was possible to remove the chair screws from the timber by hand at several locations. There was evidence of thread inserts having been used but these were ineffective. There was some elongation of the screw holes in the timber.

58. The timbers supporting the down line were removed from the troughs and cross section samples were taken from each of the sections. These samples were examined by a timber expert from TRADA Technology Limited (TTL). The timber was untreated Douglas Fir. All the sections were suffering from fungal decay which was severe enough to leave very little mechanical strength in the decayed portions. Several fractures were present in the timber. Photograph 10 shows a cross section through the longitudinal wheeltimber.

59. Three tie bars had been fitted to the down line at the east end of bridge 799 to hold the track to gauge. A tie bar is an adjustable rod that hooks onto the foot of each rail and can be tightened to hold the rails to gauge. One of these tie bars had been correctly fitted. The locknuts on the remaining two tie bars were incorrectly fitted. Tie bars are used as a temporary measure to restore track to gauge prior to undertaking permanent repairs.

The speed of the train

60. The evidence indicates that the train involved in the accident was travelling in excess of that permitted for a freight train over the route where the accident occurred. There are two factors that influenced the permitted speed of the train at the location of the accident.

61. Railtrack have a system for specifying the maximum axle weight permitted on each part of the rail network. The Railtrack Route Assessment Matrix is used to determine this weight, which generates an "RA" rating for the section of track concerned. The maximum "RA" rating is RA10. The rear eight wagons of the train were assessed as "heavy". This meant that the train could only pass over track with an RA10 rating.

62. The route between Lee and Crayford is an RA8 route. However, a process existed for permitting routes to carry individual trains with heavier axle loads than their RA rating. This process required an assessment of the route by a structural engineer. This route had been assessed previously. This resulted in a "heavy" or RA10 load being permitted passage on this route. This process generates a form BR 29973 "Advice to train crews". This is issued to the driver with relevant limitations. The speed of the train on this route was limited to 50 mph and this was stated on the form.

63. The distance between signals on Railtrack Southern Zone are designed to comply with the braking characteristics of Electric Multiple Units (EMUs). The distance an EMU requires to stop is less than that required by a freight train travelling at the same speed. The line speed for freight trains on Railtrack Southern Zone is therefore lower than for EMUs. This restriction is referred to as the "Two Thirds Rule", and where it gives rise to a lower speed limit it overrides the speed limit that is on the BR 29973 form. The line speed for passenger trains between Lee and Crayford is 60 mph, so application of the "Two Thirds Rule" gives a speed for freight trains of 40 mph. Instruction relating to the "Two Thirds Rule" are contained in a document called the "Railtrack Sectional Appendix", which is issued on a personal basis to all train drivers.

64. Based on the evidence available from the train describer download and braking calculations made by BRR the train was travelling between 51 to 59 mph.

65. The brake selector switch in the front cab of the leading locomotive was set for passenger operation rather than freight. This would have had a minimal effect on the braking capacity of the train and did not contribute to the accident.

Investigation of the overspeeding of the train

66. The maximum permitted speed of the train over the Dartford Loop was 40 mph. The speed that the train was travelling at the time of the accident was estimated to be between 51 and 59 mph. BRR estimated the speed at the point of derailment at approximately 51 mph based on a simple braking calculation for the train. This included a number of assumptions which may reduce the accuracy of the calculation. The average speed of the train through the signalling section approaching Bexley was calculated by Railtrack Southern as 59 mph. This was based on a train describer download from the signalling system records. A further calculation of the speed of the train through a 20 mph temporary speed restriction at Sidcup Station shows that the train travelled through it at approximately 28 mph.

67. The accuracy of the speedometers of the train locomotives were checked following the accident. The speedometers were found to be under-reading by an amount which increased with speed.

MPH	Speedometer Reading	(MPH)
	No 1 CAB	No 2 CAB
10	10	11
20	20	19
30	29	28
40	36	36
50	45	44
60	53	52
70	61	60

Locomotive 37167 Speedometer test following incident before repairs carried out

68. The driver was aware of the 50 mph speed restriction on train 6Y56. Form BR 29973 stated the speed. He was unaware of the 40 mph restriction or "Two Thirds Rule" listed in the Sectional Appendix. He had been trained as British Railways employee at Norwood. The investigation concluded that this was a particular problem with Drivers qualifying at Norwood not having been taught the "Two Thirds Rule".

69. The effect of the speed on the accident is difficult to assess. The passage of a train over a section of track produces horizontal and lateral forces. These forces are affected by the speed of the train and any track irregularities. The forces imposed by a

vehicle travelling between 51 to 59 mph will be greater on average than the same vehicle travelling at 40 mph. However it is not possible to calculate the difference, if any, in the forces which would have been imposed at the actual point of derailment. It is safe to say that the additional speed may have made some contribution to the accident. The additional speed will without doubt have increased the amount of damage caused by the accident.

Investigation of the cause of the gauge spread

70. Following the initial site investigations, HMRI obtained copies of records relating to track condition prior to the accident. The maintenance contract between Railtrack and SEIMCL require a hierarchy of regular inspections of the track to be carried out. The inspections include the track over Bridge 799. The relevant inspections laid down in the contract and specified in Railtrack Group Standards are;

    a. Weekly by patrollers who examine the track and its fixings.

    b. Eight-weekly by the section manager or assistant who examine the track, its fixings and make a superficial examination of the condition of the wheeltimbers.

    c. Annual examination of longitudinal wheeltimbers by a bridge examiner

    d. Two yearly examination by the Permanent Way Maintenance Engineer (PWME).

71. In addition to the track inspections carried out by SEIMCL, Railtrack uses a special rail vehicle as part of its system for monitoring the condition of the railway infrastructure. This vehicle is called the High Speed Track Recording Coach (HSTRC).

72. The patroller's inspections reports identified "Rotten wheeltimbers tie bars fitted" (9/9/96); "Bridge timbers Very bad condition" (7/11/96); "wheel timber needs changing (urgently)" (17/12/96); and "Extremely rotten bridge timber requires urgent attention" (22/1/97).

73. The section manager and assistant's inspection reports identified "Wheel timber needs renewing urgent" (27/2/96); "Bridge 799 1450 gauge, new sleepers required. cut back flying ends. 6 foot timber urgent twist on bridge tie bars cannot be fitted - programmed urgent" (16/8/96); and "New 6 foot timber req. urgent twist on bridge, tie bars cannot be fitted - programmed urgent" (25/11/96).

74. The Permanent Way Maintenance Engineer's (PWME) report of January 1996 identified "Timbers to change Bexley".

75. Tie bars had been fitted to the country end of Bridge 799 to control the gauge widening. Tie bars are a short term measure used prior to more permanent repairs. The existence of tie bars at this location are first referred to on 9/9/96 in a patroller's

report. The patroller states that "tie bars have been fitted" and the assistant section manager's reports of 16/8/96 and 25/11/96 state that "tie bars cannot be fitted". This suggests that the tie bars were fitted at the wrong location or that tie bars were required at two separate locations to correct the gauge. The frequency of the patroller's inspection was laid down as weekly. The records confirmed a frequency of approximately two weekly. The inspection frequencies attained by the section manager and his assistant of both the track and specialist inspections were 3 to 4 monthly and not 8 weekly as prescribed in Railtrack standards .

76.   Longitudinal wheeltimbers are recognised as a "weak point" in the track support structure that may be prone to failure if not adequately inspected and maintained. Appendix 4 lists 15 of the derailments that have occurred on longitudinal wheeltimber bridges since 1/1/88. All these derailments have been caused by gauge spread.

77.   Railtrack Standards address this increased risk by requiring a detailed examination of the timber integrity by a competent person on an annual basis. The examination of the longitudinal wheeltimbers on Bridge 799 formed part of the RT1A contract. These inspections were carried out by Balfour Beatty Rail Projects on behalf of SEIMCL.

78.   The bridge examiner undertook an inspection on 13/8/95 and identified "No 10, Severe Decay To Country/end of Timber.....Also Country/end of Timber No 7......Remainder:- Large Splits & Shakes Throughout. With Rail Chairs Sinking Approx 5 mm". The report is countersigned by the Examination Manager "Spot renewal 2nd Qtr 96/97" (3/10/95 and by the Permanent Way Maintenance Engineer "Agreed" (16/10/95). The 2nd quarter 96/97 refers to the period July to September 1996.

79.   The Bridge Examiner undertook an inspection on 13/8/96 and identified "Timbers no 7 & 10 in poor condition. severe decay occur throughout....Remaining timbers:- large splits and shakes throughout. 1995 Recommendations:- spot renewals 2nd quarter 96/97." Timbers 7 and 10 approximate lifespan is described as "Expired".

80.   In December 1996 a longitudinal wheeltimber replacement programme produced by a consultant working for SEIMCL identified the urgent need to replace all the existing timbers on Bridge 799 down line. A date on which the lines could be closed to enable the replacement work to be carried out was identified for the weekend of 11th/12th January 1997. Unfortunately, because of poor organisation and a breakdown in communication within SEIMCL, no-one arranged for the work to be done.

81.   The HSTRC records the geometry of the track using measuring equipment and on board computers. This includes vertical and horizontal alignment, twist and gauge. Any irregularities that exceed specified maxima are recorded as Level 2 exceedences. HMRI obtained copies of these for the previous six consecutive runs for the section of track where the accident occurred. There had been Level 2 exceedences in both twist and gauge on every one of these runs in the vicinity of Bridge 799. The absolute location of these defects varied slightly, but the relative locations indicate two twist faults and one gauge fault. The investigation concluded that the country end of

Bridge 799 is the location of the gauge fault. The two twist faults being located 2 to 3 yards and 11 to 12 yards prior to the gauge defect. This information was provided by Railtrack to SEIMCL.

82. The SEIMCL contract area covers the whole of Kent and is split into three sections. One of these is called the Kent Link area and includes the Dartford Loop. The Permanent Way Maintenance Engineer (Kent Link) heads the part of the organisation responsible for maintaining the track in this area. Between 10th May 1996 and 14th August 1996 this post was vacant. Some cover was arranged, but the bulk of the post's responsibilities went unattended. In the later part of 1996, and early in 1997, SEIMCL were engaged in a major restructuring of staff in the maintenance and inspection organisation. After the PWME's post was filled on 14th August 1996 matters were still not fully resolved as the individual in the Kent Link post was responsible for the reorganisation not only of the Kent Link area, but the Kent Coast area as well. The new incumbent realised that because of the workload created by reorganisation he was unable to properly fulfil the requirements of the post which related to the safety of the railway. He obtained the assistance of a contract permanent way consultant for a brief period during December 1996. He specifically instructed the consultant to examine the annual longitudinal wheeltimber inspections for the Kent Link area. This was done, but no action was taken by SEIMCL staff to allocate resources and to plan the work in any further detail.

83. In conclusion the track was in a very poor state of repair. The longitudinal wheeltimbers had been identified by all track inspection staff, the bridge examiners, and the HSTRC as warranting a detailed inspection and follow up works. SEIMCL failed to take action to repair the track and its supports. Railtrack ignored the HSTRC output over a period in excess of 18 months and so failed to monitor SEIMCL's performance or to take appropriate action to ensure the safety of the track.

Investigation of the overloading of the wagons

84. The first 12 wagons in the train were weighed at Hoo Junction following the derailment. The 12th wagon (PR 3001), which was the only loaded wagon not to have shed its load weighed 121.32 tonnes. It was a 102t GLW bogie box wagon with a load capacity of 69 tonnes. The measured load was actually 88.32 tonnes which represents a substantial overloading of 28%.

85. These wagons had originally been supplied for transporting steel to and from Sheerness. More recently they had been used for carrying ballast to and from track renewals sites. The wagons have a large volumetric capacity, which allows for gross overloading if they are filled with dense material.

86. Wagon PR 3001 had formed part of train 8Z24 which travelled over the weekend of 1/2 February from Eastleigh to Three Bridges via a STRCL renewals site between Billingshurst and Pulborough, Sussex. The wagon was empty when it left Eastleigh on Friday 31st January. It was loaded with spoil from the renewal site during the course of the weekend possession and left the renewals site for Three Bridges depot on the morning of Sunday 2nd February, over a route which included track rated at

RA 7. Because of this STRCL site supervisors had been instructed to load the box wagons to 75% capacity.

87. The investigation found that this downgrading of the maximum load carried by the wagons was not based on sound judgement. It seems that the assumption was made that when a wagon is full its load is equal to the maximum carrying capacity of the vehicle. This ignores the difference in density of different materials. STRCL did have information on the density of both new ballast and spoil. A test weighing of new ballast in a 102T GLW wagon with a volume of 53.1 cubic metres had been undertaken in October 1994. The density of new ballast, 1.6 tonne/m^3 was extrapolated to give a spoil density of 1.88 tonne/m^3. Based on this figure reducing the load carried by the wagon to 75% capacity would have resulted in a load of over 90 tonnes. This exceeds by over 30% the load capacity of both the wagon and track rated at RA 10.

88. The investigation concluded that PR 3001 was grossly overloaded. The overloaded wagon would have in general imposed increased vertical and lateral forces on the track. The poorly maintained track over Bridge 799 was already weak and the additional forces imposed by the wagon caused the track to finally collapse.

Investigation of the movement of the wheels on their axles

89. The examination of the wheelsets was carried out by BRR and monitored by HSE's Health and Safety Laboratory. Interested parties including CAIB UK Ltd and Tiphook were invited to attend.

90. The four wheelsets were visually examined. In all four cases the nearside (in the direction of travel) wheel had moved inwards on the axle. In one case the wheel had moved completely off the wheelseat and was loose. This examination revealed no evidence of the wheels having moved prior to the derailment occurring. All damage was consistent with a derailment.

91. The axleboxes and bearings were examined. No unusual features were found. All the bearings were adequately greased. The axleboxes had suffered some damage which was consistent with a derailment.

92. The wheel flange height and thickness were all within tolerance. The seven wheels that remained on their wheelseats were back pressure tested to test the fit of the wheels on their axles. The wheel bore and axle wheelseat dimensions for all the wheels on these four axles were measured.

93. BRR were of the opinion that it is unusual to find that a wheel has moved on its axle wheelseat following a derailment. The force required to move a wheel on its wheelseat is considerable. However, the derailment occurred on railway arches approximately eight metres high. This resulted in the wagons (except the 12th wagon) falling a considerable distance. Given that there was no evidence of any lack of wheel to wheelseat fit and having reviewed the results of the back pressure tests and other measurements taken following the derailment BRR concluded that the force of impact will have caused the wheels to move on the wheelseats. The movement of

the wheels on the axles was a direct result of the incident and could not have been a cause of the derailment.

SAFETY MANAGEMENT OVERVIEW

The condition of the track

94. Railtrack, as infrastructure owner and controller, makes its track, and associated structures, available to the operators of trains. Employees and members of the public may be put at significant risk if this infrastructure is not properly maintained.

95. These obligations are formalised in Railtrack's Railway Safety Case. Under the Railways (Safety Case) Regulations 1994, brought into place to ensure railway safety following the privatisation of British Rail, Railtrack had to prepare and have accepted by HSE a Railway Safety Case (RSC). This describes how Railtrack will conduct its operations to ensure an acceptable level of safety and includes the arrangements for maintenance of the infrastructure.

96. Railtrack employed SEIMCL to maintain the track at the accident location. The infrastructure maintenance contract, known as the RT1A contract includes a specification for the level of track quality the contractor has to achieve. The RSC (see Appendix 2) clearly outlines the role Railtrack play in ensuring that their contractor meets this specification.

97. In the winter of 1995/96 HMRI undertook an in-depth inspection exercise which looked in a thorough and concerted way at the management systems put in place by Railtrack to secure the safety of the national railway infrastructure. In particular the exercise looked at Railtrack's arrangements for selection, monitoring and control of its contractors. The exercise identified a number of weaknesses in Railtrack's management of its contractors and a potential risk to the safety of the national railway infrastructure. HSE published a report of their major findings. Extracts from the report; "Maintaining a Safe Railway Infrastructure", can be found in Appendix 7.

98. HSE also issued an Improvement Notice requiring an improved Railtrack strategy for Monitoring Contractors' Performance. The schedule to this notice can be found in Appendix 8. This describes the actions HSE required Railtrack to take in order to comply with the notice.

99. The strategy adopted by Railtrack involved audit of management systems and site checks or end product checks (the physical outcome of the contractor's activity). The strategy was risk based. A number of related Railtrack procedures were introduced as part of this.

100. The HSE accident investigation found very little evidence of the new standards having been implemented before the accident. Railtrack were unable to produce an audit plan for the 12 months leading up to the accident, although some audits had been carried out. Railtrack were unable to produce an end product checks plan. No evidence of end product checks having been carried out was found. The resources

available to the Railtrack Permanent Way Engineer were insufficient to enable the end product checks to be done

101. The Railtrack Zone where the accident occurred; Southern Zone, was created by a merger of the former South and South West Zones on 11th November 1996. This resulted in a number of changes in personnel between that date and 4th February 1997. Following the merger of Railtrack South and South West Zones to form Southern Zone, there was evidence of measures being taken to address the lack of an audit or end product check plan. However these had not yet been implemented.

The condition of the vehicles

102. The wagons were owned by either CAIB UK Ltd or Tiphook Ltd. The wagons were leased to STRCL to carry stone to or spoil from renewals sites. At the time of the accident at Bridge 799, the wagons that formed train 6Y56 were operated by English, Welsh and Scottish Railways who are a company owned by Wisconsin Central Transportation Ltd. English, Welsh and Scottish Railways had hired a Connex South Central train crew to operate the train between Three Bridges and Hoo Junction.

103. English, Welsh and Scottish Railways as an operator of freight trains has the responsibility to ensure that wagons travelling on the rail network are appropriately loaded to conform with both the carrying capacity of the wagon and the route over which the wagon passes. STRCL as a contractor loading a freight wagon has a similar responsibility.

104. This responsibility is both part of the Health and Safety at Work etc. Act 1974 Section 3(1), which outlines an employer's duties to those other than their employees and the Railways (Safety Case) Regulations 1994, which require a train operator to hold a Railway Safety Case (RSC). EWS as a train operator holds a RSC which is accepted by Railtrack. STRCL hold a RSC both as a train operator and as a contractor, which are accepted by Railtrack. The RSCs in these cases did not adequately address the areas of risk associated with overloading vehicles.

LEGAL PROCEEDINGS

105. HSE decided to institute proceedings against Railtrack plc, SEIMCL and STRCL because it was concluded that it was the management failures of these companies which were the main cause of the accident.

106. The case was first heard at Bexley Magistrates' Court on 26 May 1998. In view of the seriousness of the offences the charges were referred to the Crown Court to be heard on indictment.

107. On 7 September 1998 at Kingston Crown Court Railtrack plc, SEIMCL and STRCL pleaded guilty to the following charges:

   a)   Railtrack plc - failing to ensure, so far as was reasonably practicable, that persons not in their employment were not exposed to risks to their safety in that the track on the down line at Bridge 799 between Bexley and Crayford

Railway Stations was not in a safe condition for the passage of trains contrary to Section 3(1) of the Health and Safety at Work etc. Act 1974.

b)   SEIMCL - failing to ensure, so far as was reasonably practicable, that persons not in their employment were not exposed to risks to their safety in that they failed to maintain the down line track and its supports at Bridge 799 between Bexley and Crayford Railway Stations in a safe condition, contrary to Section 3(1) of the Health and Safety at Work etc. Act 1974.

c)   STRCL - failing to ensure, so far as was reasonably practicable, that persons not their your employment were not exposed to risks to their safety in that they failed to ensure that the wagons which they loaded at your track renewals site between Billingshurst and Pulborough Railway Stations were not loaded beyond the safe carrying capacity of the route they were to travel over, contrary to Section 3(1) of the Health and Safety at Work etc. Act 1974.

108.   All parties pleaded guilty to the offences. The overall fine was £150,000. This fine was apportioned based on the assessment of the culpability of each particular company by the judge and two magistrates. SEIMCL was fined 55% of this total (£82,500). Railtrack plc was fined 40% (£60,000). STRCL was fined 5% (£7,500). HSE was awarded costs of £41,768. These were apportioned on the same basis.

109.   In his sentencing remarks the judge stated that it "was *merciful that nobody was killed although four people were injured*." He also stated that in his and the two magistrates' view *"Railtrack has the overall responsibility of protecting the public from any failures of its contractors STR and SEI. It is clear that they failed to heed the warning issued in the document "Maintaining a safe railway infrastructure". It set itself high standards in its document "Railtrack's Railway Safety Case" and it has failed in our view to attain them."*

CONCLUSION AND LESSONS TO BE LEARNT

110.   The accident at Bexley had an immediate impact on all those involved in terms of serious injuries and damage to the railway infrastructure and businesses located in the railway arches at Bexley. The longer term impact includes financial losses, damaging public relations and protracted and costly civil and criminal cases. The immediate and underlying causes of the accident contain many vital lessons. Possibly more important is the emphasis placed on these conclusions and lessons to be learnt by others in the industry.

111.   The HMRI investigation identified a number of lessons to be learnt. These are not restricted to those companies involved in the accident. The purpose in publishing this report is to stimulate all those in the railway industry to improve their safety management. The lessons to be learnt have been made on a company by company basis to reflect the structure of the railway industry. HSE recommends that other Railtrack zones, infrastructure maintenance contractors, track renewal contractors and train operating companies should examine their own business or part of their business and ensure that the failings of those involved at Bexley are not their failings too.

Lessons to be learnt by infrastructure maintenance contractors

112.   The HSE investigation concluded that the condition of the track at the time of the derailment was the most significant factor in causing this accident. SEIMCL had no plans at the time of the accident to replace the longitudinal wheeltimbers. This was in spite of the inspections carried out by patrollers, the section manager and assistant section manager and bridge examiner having identified the urgent need to do so. An independent consultant employed by SEIMCL had also identified the need to replace the wheeltimbers.

113.   Individuals within the SEIMCL organisation were aware that there were works that required planning, but failed to take any action, relying on those at a more senior level to ensure the necessary progress. It was unclear who was responsible for progressing the replacement of the longitudinal wheeltimbers. The role of the Permanent Way Maintenance Engineer (PWME) was crucial in this respect as the most senior individual with any form of "hands on" knowledge of the area. The PWME's post was either vacant or filled on a temporary basis between May 1996 to August 1996. The PWME who took over on 10th August 1996 did not do so on a permanent basis. He retained some responsibility for his previous area, and had an additional workload because the company were also restructuring the track maintenance function.

114.   There was no clear and consistent procedure for ensuring works were undertaken or identification of who was responsible for championing the work.

Lesson 1

It is essential that each contractor responsible for maintaining the railway infrastructure in a safe condition should have clear systems to ensure they achieve this.

Lesson 2

Each infrastructure maintenance company should identify and provide the resource required both to manage and to implement these systems.

---

115.   The individuals managing and implementing these systems and those carrying out the work should be aware of and understand them. They should be competent to carry out the tasks required of them. "Competence" means that employees must have the necessary skills, experience, knowledge and personal qualities required to do the job. The demands of the task should not exceed the individual's ability to carry it out.

Lesson 3

Each infrastructure maintenance company should ensure that staff are competent to carry out the tasks required of them without undue risk to themselves or others.

---

116. All organisations change and it is intrinsic in good management that an organisation reacts to this change by recognising it and dealing with it effectively. Change generates a workload in terms of tasks to be undertaken. This may be a change in staffing levels, movement of staff, method of carrying out work, changes in systems, procedures, organisational structures etc. This change in turn introduces new risks. SEIMCL are in an accelerated process of change following privatisation of the railway industry. This change is internally and externally driven. The impact of additional workload generated by this change was not adequately assessed.

117. In particular SEIMCL failed to assess the impact of the changes both the company and the industry were experiencing and to manage the change. The HSE publication "Successful Health and Safety Management" (HSG65) details how an organisation can control their health and safety risks. The guidance includes:

> how to set policy that fulfils the spirit and the letter of the law,
> how to organise by promoting and sustaining a positive safety culture,
> how to plan and implement an effective health and safety management system
>   by minimising risk,
> how to measure performance both actively and reactively, and
> how to learn from experience by monitoring and reviewing performance.

Lesson 4

Each infrastructure maintenance company should undertake ongoing monitoring and reassessment to confirm the adequacy of the systems and resource provided. Modifications to systems or resources should be made as necessary.

---

118. The Health and Safety at Work etc. Act 1974 requires employers to assess and control the risks arising from their undertaking. SEIMCL failed to do this adequately.

Lessons to be learnt by Railtrack zones and headquarters

119. Railtrack as the owners and controllers of the infrastructure must ensure that the infrastructure is maintained in a safe condition. In contracting out the maintenance of the infrastructure, Railtrack need to monitor the performance of their contractors and the condition of the infrastructure. It is therefore vital that Railtrack have a strategy to achieve this and implement it.

120. In late 1995 HMRI undertook an intrusive audit of Railtrack. In March 1996 HSE published a report of the findings of this audit; "Maintaining a safe railway infrastructure". The report identified ten key action points for Railtrack. The Executive Summary and Principal Findings of this report are contained in Appendix 7. Following publication of this report HSE issued two Improvement Notices on Railtrack. The notices required Railtrack;

1.   to comply with their own safety case, and
2.   to produce an improved strategy for monitoring its contractors' performance, and an implementation plan for the elements of that strategy.

121.   In response to the Improvement Notices Railtrack produced a procedure; "Contract Performance Monitoring Strategy" and an implementation plan. This met the requirements of the second notice. Railtrack South latterly Railtrack Southern failed to implement this strategy. They failed to undertake the majority of the management system audits (office based checks) or end product checks (site based checks) prescribed in their strategy. This meant that they were unaware of the adequacy of the performance of their contractor and so failed to ensure that SEIMCL were complying with standards of maintenance set by Railtrack.

122.   The resource needed to implement the strategy was not identified or provided.

Lesson 5

It is essential that each Railtrack Zone implements the Railtrack "Contract Performance Monitoring Strategy". The resource required to implement and maintain this strategy should be identified and provided.

Lesson 6

The individuals managing and implementing the "Contract Performance Monitoring Strategy" should be competent to do so.

---

123.   A key element of the strategy is to assess the results of monitoring undertaken and target future inspections on a risk based approach. This approach addresses the risks that arise as a result of the continuous process of change that all organisations are subject to. The approach is in accordance with the HSE publication "Successful Health and Safety Management" (HSG65) referred to in paragraph 118.

124.   Railtrack were in possession of the HSTRC data for the track between Lee and Crayford covering a period of at least 18 months prior to the accident. Railtrack had identified the HSTRC as a tool for monitoring the condition of the infrastructure. The information from these runs recorded serious safety defects in the vicinity of Bridge 799 at Bexley. Railtrack failed to take any action to rectify these defects or the contractor's failures.

125.   Railtrack not only failed to implement the "Contract Performance Monitoring Strategy", but also to review its implementation and effectiveness. They failed to review adequately whether they were succeeding in ensuring that the railway infrastructure was maintained in a safe condition.

Lesson 7

Each Railtrack Zone should ensure that they undertake ongoing monitoring and reassessment of their contractors performance in accordance with the "Contract Performance Monitoring Strategy".

Lesson 8

Railtrack Zones and Railtrack headquarters should monitor and review the effectiveness of the systems they have in place to ensure that the infrastructure is maintained in a safe condition. They should monitor and review the adequacy of the resource provided to undertake this.

126. An intrinsic part of ensuring that the infrastructure is maintained in a safe condition is to have a procedure to address the contractor's failure to perform.

Lesson 9

Railtrack should ensure that they have adequate systems and procedures to not only identify failures by their contractor to maintain the infrastructure adequately but to ensure these failures are rectified.

127. Railtrack as the owner and controller of the railway infrastructure permitted the overloaded and speeding freight train access to the railway. Railtrack determined the permitted safe axle weight and speed of the train across the routes it travelled, but they failed to monitor what was actually happening on the railway. Those using the railway had overloaded the train that derailed at Bexley and driven it in excess of the line speed.

Lesson 10

Railtrack should undertake ongoing monitoring and reassessment of those using their infrastructure to ensure they do so safely.

128. More specifically Railtrack failed to ensure that their track renewals contractor; STRCL loaded the wagons correctly. The use of large box type wagons that can be overloaded not only above the route carrying capacity of a particular line, but also above their own carrying capacity poses a significant risk. The accident at Bexley demonstrates this very clearly.

129. The wagons were loaded by STRCL, hauled by EWS and the locomotive driven by Connex South Central. There was clearly potential for confusion over responsibilities of each party in the loading and preparation of the train.

Lesson 11

Railtrack with the track renewals and train operating companies should review the effectiveness of existing control measures for ensuring that wagons are not loaded in excess of the route carrying capacity and then moved over the railway infrastructure. The revisions identified should be implemented.

---

130. The Health and Safety at Work etc. Act 1974 requires employers to assess and control the risks arising from their undertaking. Railtrack failed to do this adequately.

Lessons to be learnt by track renewals companies

131. STRCL, whose staff loaded the wagons on their renewals site between Billingshurst and Pulborough, failed to assess adequately the load that would be imposed on the wagons and the track. They failed to make a simple calculation. If this had been done it would have been obvious that the wagon would be overloaded at 75% of its volumetric capacity.

132. The checks made of the wagons, when loaded, by both STRCL and the train operating companies were insufficient. The system/procedures identified individuals with insufficient training or expertise to inspect the loads carried by the wagons. The large box type wagons involved in the accident at Bexley were introduced as spoil wagons comparatively recently (1990). Their large capacity poses a particular risk of overloading when using dense materials.

Lesson 12

The track renewals companies in conjunction with the train operating companies and Railtrack should evaluate the risks to both rolling stock and infrastructure of overloaded wagons. They should produce and implement a more robust system for assessing the load carried by a wagon and ensuring that load does not exceed specified levels.

---

134. The Health and Safety at Work etc. Act 1974 requires employers to assess and control the risks arising from their undertaking. STRCL failed to do this adequately.

Lessons to be learnt by train operating companies

135. A substantial risk existed of train 6Y56 derailing as it travelled over Bridge 799 at the appropriate line speed of 40 mph. The additional speed of the train will have imparted additional forces to the track, but as stated earlier the contribution this may have made to the accident is not clear.

136. The two causes of the trains excess speed were the driver's lack of knowledge of the "Two Thirds Rule" and the under-reading speedometer.

137. The driver had been trained at Norwood depot and stated that he had not been taught the "Two Thirds Rule". This restricted freight trains to two thirds of line speed on Southern Zone routes. The evidence suggests that the driver's lack of knowledge resulted from an historical failure to adequately train the driver by British Rail prior to privatisation of the rail network.

138. However, the Railway (Safety Critical Work) Regulations 1994 state that no employer shall permit any of his employees to undertake safety critical work unless the employee is competent. It is not sufficient simply to train an individual to undertake a task. A training and competence assessment must be made of drivers on a regular basis, which includes further training if necessary. This must include monitoring the individual at work.

Lesson 13

Train operating companies should have a system for ongoing reassessment of the competence of their drivers, which includes periodic retraining and on the job assessment. This system should be maintained.

---

139. The driver had been advised via the issue of form BR29973 that the permitted line speed of train 6Y56 was 50 mph. The driver stated that he had never seen the reverse of form BR29973, which includes speed restrictions over certain bridges, junctions etc. The investigation found that it is common practice for these forms to be faxed to drivers, which leads to only the front side of the notice being received. In this case this did not contribute to the accident.

140. The failure to issue the driver with the reverse of form BR 29973 may have resulted in his exceeding the speed limit elsewhere on his journey. The risks that arose did not result in a derailment. However, the risk of a derailment earlier in the train's journey is obvious.

Lesson 14

Train operating companies should ensure that drivers are both aware of the information they should be receiving and that it is received. The effectiveness of the system to achieve this should be monitored.

---

141. The under-reading speedometer will have contributed to the overspeeding of the train. Since the accident EWS have increased the frequency at which speedometers are checked.

Lesson 15

Train operating companies should review the frequency at which locomotive or train speedometers are inspected.

Management of the accident site

142. The accident occurred in a populated area of South East London.

143. It was Railtrack's task to manage the accident site alongside the emergency services. The emergency services responded well to the accident. Problems were encountered by both Railtrack, the emergency services and HMRI in having to deal with the large number of different railway personnel and companies who attended the accident site. This had the potential to give rise to confusion. Railtrack worked well with British Transport Police and the other emergency services to ensure the co-ordination and control of all the railway representatives present. Regular meetings were held to ensure the effective management of the incident site.

ACTIONS TAKEN

144. The lessons learnt following this derailment have been acknowledged by the companies involved. It is essential that these lessons and actions taken should be noted by all the railway industry. It is possible that further accidents may then be avoided with similar underlying causes The Health and Safety at Work etc. Act 1974 and associated regulations require employers to manage their undertaking safely. It is this underlying failure by those involved that caused this accident. Specific failures in the process did not in themselves cause the accident.

145. As a result of the accident Railtrack Southern convened a formal inquiry which produced a report of their findings. The report made a number of recommendations which addressed some of the general and specific failings of those involved. HMRI were provided with a copy of this report and have examined it. The implementation of the recommendations has been reviewed by HMRI and will be subject to follow up action.

146. Some actions have been taken to address the lessons to be learnt identified by HMRI. These actions are described below. HMRI will continue to monitor the response of those involved in the accident and of others in the railway industry. HMRI have set up a national project on track standards and have been proactive in raising both the setting and implementation of standards, the actual standards achieved and the measures to raise standards. Formal enforcement action has been and will continue to be considered where appropriate.

Actions taken to address lessons 1, 2, 3 and 4

147. Following the accident SEIMCL undertook a significant review of how they met the requirements of the RT1A track maintenance contract for the south eastern part of the Railtrack Southern zone.

    1.   They reviewed their work planning procedures to ensure that they were comprehensive, understood by all concerned and existed in writing.

    2.   They reviewed the adequacy of their resource (quantity and quality) in respect of deputising arrangements, track inspections and urgent track maintenance work.

    3.   They reviewed the adequacy of instruction and guidance currently provided to staff in respect of what constitutes unsafe track, and the standards of maintenance appropriate in a given situation.

148. Based on the information provided, HMRI believe the review undertaken by SEIMCL was comprehensive.

149. In the future SEIMCL should continue to review how they meet the requirements of the RT1A contract safely. Railtrack should continue to monitor their contractor and ensure that he maintains the railway infrastructure in a safe manner.

150. HMRI will continue to examine SEIMCL's and other infrastructure maintenance contractor's compliance with health and safety legislation and regulation.

Actions taken to address lessons 5, 6, 7, 8, and 9

151. Following the accident at Bexley Railtrack Southern undertook an immediate review of Southern zone procedures for auditing their infrastructure maintenance contractor. Revised check procedures were produced and implemented.

152. More recently (August 1998) Railtrack headquarters commissioned a national review of their procedures for auditing their infrastructure maintenance contractors by an independent consultant. This review is intended to identify current best practice, recommend refinements to existing procedures and to design and deliver a series of training courses to Zone and headquarters staff.

153. HMRI are of the opinion that Railtrack headquarters understand the concerns outlined in the HMRI report "Maintaining a safe railway infrastructure" and are actively seeking to address them. Railtrack headquarters have over the last 12 months paid particular attention to the implementation of the "Contract Performance Monitoring Strategy". They are actively monitoring the zones compliance with the strategy and the adequacy of the resource.

154. It is vital that all Railtrack zones also understand the concerns outlined in the HMRI report and are fully committed to and adequately resourced to implement and maintain the "Contract Performance Monitoring Strategy".

Actions taken to address lessons 10 and 11

155.   Following the accident at Bexley a cross industry working group was established to review the use of box wagons for carrying spent ballast. Railtrack were part of the working group. Railtrack Safety and Standards Directorate in conjunction with this working group developed a process of "Certificates of Readiness" for engineering trains and "fitness to travel" for wagons leaving sites. This is intended to clearly identify the responsibilities of the various parties involved in the loading and preparation of engineering trains.

156.   The assessment and monitoring of loaded wagons with coil suspensions was considered by Railtrack following the Bexley accident. Railtrack have since purchased 15 portable wagon weighing devices. These were brought into use in May 1998 across the railway network.

157.   HMRI will be assessing the effectiveness of these measures.

Actions taken to address lessons 12

158.   STRCL and EWS placed a 50% loading limit on all big box wagons following the accident at Bexley. A 50% load line was painted inside the boxes. This was a reactive short term measure.

159.   The cross industry working group referred to in paragraph 155 assessed the density of different types of spoil that might be loaded into these big box wagons. The results have been used to form the basis of loading instructions to staff working with freight traffic.

160.   A documented handover system between the contractor loading the wagons and the train operator hauling the train was set-up by Railtrack as described in paragraph 155.

161.   The 50% loading restriction of box wagons was lifted in September 1998 following the completion of fitting load indicators and briefing of staff in the instructions for their use.

162.   HMRI will be assessing the effectiveness of these load indicators as a control measure.

Actions taken to address lesson 13

163.   Connex South Central are currently reviewing their driver training arrangements and standards. A revised driver training course is proposed to be introduced in November 1998. The matter is subject to a revision to the Connex South Central Safety Case, which is approved by Railtrack. This Safety Case submission will be reviewed by HMRI.

164.   EWS revised their Safety Critical Work assessment package for drivers in December 1996 to include the "Two Thirds Rule". In June 1998 they introduced a revised

Company Standard Acquisition and Retention of Route Knowledge. They have also developed a Traincrew Basic Training course that was implemented in August 1998.

Actions taken to address lesson 14

165. Connex South Central have withdrawn from the contract to provide drivers for freight trains to EWS railways.

166. EWS are developing their own replacement for the TOPS system. This is a system that is able to provide the driver with information relating to his train, the load it carries and the route it is to travel over.

Actions taken to address lesson 15

167. In mid 1997 EWS changed from the British Rail inherited system of only checking speedometer equipment at tyre turning to a system of planned checks based on the number of hours in traffic.

FURTHER ACTION

168. HMRI will be writing to the companies involved and requiring them to provide an updated response to the lessons to be learnt contained in this report within two months of the date of issue. Inspectors from HMRI will ensure that these responses describe how each company has translated the lessons learnt into actions and describe the work undertaken or propose a timescale for completion of any further work that arises. The need for further enforcement action will be assessed by HMRI.

169. HMRI are continuing to follow up a number of specific areas that relate to this report. These include:
1.   An investigation of the effectiveness of the control measures used to ensure safe loading of box wagons on renewals sites and onward movement on the rail network.
2.   Monitoring the progressive implementation of the "Contract Performance Monitoring Strategy" by Railtrack Zones.
3.   Railtrack have recently submitted to HMRI a major revision to their Railway Safety Case as a result of a three yearly review required by the regulations. Following some amendments made by Railtrack we have accepted this safety case. We will continue to monitor their performance against this safety case.
4.   The Railtrack Railway Safety Case specifies Railtrack Group Standards as a key part of the safety management process. These standards were largely inherited from British Rail. Railtrack are reviewing these standards. There is a process of consultation by Railtrack and we are commenting as appropriate.

Appendices

Class 37 diesel locomotive 37167
Class 37 diesel locomotive 37220

Wagon Number	TOPS code	Loaded/empty	Actual weight recorded (tonnes) and comments
7067900411	JRA	Loaded	34.36 - 10-15% new ballast
PR 3202	KEA	Loaded	52.92 - 40% mixed new and old
PR 3167	JNA	Empty	35.36 - 5% mixed new and old
PR 3241	KEA	Empty	31.84 - <5% mixed new and old sand
PR 3230	KEA	Empty	41.76 - 10% new and sand
PR 3224	KEA	Empty	38.52 - 10% new and sand
PR 3237	KEA	Empty	35.68 - 5% new and sand
PR 3183	KEA	Empty	31.12 - near empty
PR 3211	KEA	Empty	28.48 - near empty
7067900759	JRA	Loaded	24.96 - near empty
CAIB 3255	JNA	Loaded	55.92 - part loaded new ballast
PR 3001	JXA	Loaded	121.32 - loaded spoil - derailed
PR 3002	JXA	Loaded	derailed
PR 3003	JXA	Loaded	derailed
PR 3007	JXA	Loaded	derailed
7067900700	JRA	Loaded	derailed
7067900726	JRA	Loaded	derailed
7067900098	JRA	Loaded	derailed
7067900254	JRA	Loaded	derailed

Total: TOPS record = 11 loaded, 8 empty wagons
          Site record = 3 empty, remainder full or partly loaded

APPENDIX 2
Extracts from Railway Safety Cases in relation to issues of safety management

From Railtrack's Safety Case 17

5.17   Railtrack has overall responsibility for the safety of all activities, on its infrastructure and is also the 'directing mind' for safety of the Railway Group.

(The Railway Group is defined within Railtrack's RSC as "the group of organisations comprising Railtrack, the duty holders of Railway Safety Cases accepted by Railtrack, and the BRB as long as it continues to own train operators".)

5.52   Railtrack owns all of the national mainline railway infrastructure. This includes; track, electrification systems, signalling, sidings, depots, stations, level crossings, and operational buildings, tunnels, viaducts, bridges and other structures.

Clause 7.26 "Railtrack is responsible for the design, installation and maintenance of track, signalling, electrification systems, level crossings and operational buildings, tunnels, viaducts, bridges and other such structures ...".

Clause 7.28 "Railtrack conforms with Railway Group Standards as mandatory technical documents".

Clause 7.29 "Railtrack achieves the maintenance, renewal and improvement of its infrastructure by the use of contractors who will be required as a condition of their contract specification to comply with the requirements of the applicable parts of Railway Group Standards or Railtrack Line Procedures, etc".

Section 7.35 "Railtrack ensures that its infrastructure contractors maintain adequate data on the condition of the infrastructure. This includes production and agreement with Railtrack on maintenance plans and renewal of the infrastructure".
Clause 7.36 "The responsibility for ensuring that the infrastructure contractors actually perform to the contract specification is that of the appropriate Zonal Senior Contracts Manager or Project Managers...." (These people are employees of Railtrack plc).

Clause 10.3.1 "A programme of planned inspections will be carried out on equipment, activities and at all locations in order to monitor condition, identify unsafe acts and to improve work efficiency".

Clause 10.3.2 "All locations which Railtrack controls are subject to a planned inspection and maintenance programme, and made the responsibility of a nominated individual".

Clause 10.3.3 "Effective systems for rectification of defects revealed by planned inspections are set up by the manager responsible for equipment activities or the location...".

Clause 10.9.11 "The extent of pro-active safety performance monitoring reflects the extent of the risks involved. For example, particular focus is given to monitoring of the safety performance of contractors, both in how they carry out their work, and the results achieved".

Clause 10.18.5 The Railtrack line has incorporated in its organisational structure posts to provide the appropriate professional engineering, procurement, contract management and project management expertise to allow them to effectively let and manage contracts.

Clause 10.18.25 "The infrastructure maintenance contracts, and new works managed by a Directorate are managed by a nominated Manager or Project Manager respectively...

Clause 10.18.26 The nominated Manager or Project Manager is the normal point of contact between Railtrack and the contractor and is responsible for ensuring, that the contractor:-

- has a validated Health and Safety Plan or Safety Plan as appropriate for the contract concerned;
- carries out his work to the performance level required by the contract;
- implements changes required as a result of health and safety and technical audits

does not import unacceptable risk as a result of his activities upon Railtrack's controlled infrastructure".

APPENDIX 3   **Photographs**

PHOTOGRAPH 2
View of the derailed wagons numbers 14 to 18 showing
Pharmax building and damage to viaduct arches looking towards
Crayford from Bridge 799.

PHOTOGRAPH 3
The rearmost 19th wagon after derailment looking towards
Crayford from Bridge 799.

PHOTOGRAPH 4
Damage to viaduct, arches and track looking
towards Crayford from Bridge 799.

PHOTOGRAPH 5
Looking back towards Bexley Station, damage to track
and derailed wagons 14 to 19.

PHOTOGRAPH 6
Looking towards Crayford showing damage to track and
the 13th wagon which came to rest at the river bridge.

PHOTOGRAPH 7
Damage to bridge over River Cray looking towards Crayford.
The derailed 13th wagon and bogies can also be seen.

PHOTOGRAPH 8
Bridge 799 from the Crayford end looking towards Lee.
The two tie bars to the front of the photograph are incorrectly fitted.

PHOTOGRAPH 9
Six foot wheeltimber looking towards Lee showing large
splits in the wheeltimber, and evidence of both lateral and vertical
movement of the baseplates on the wheeltimber.

Top surface of wheeltimber on which baseplates are located

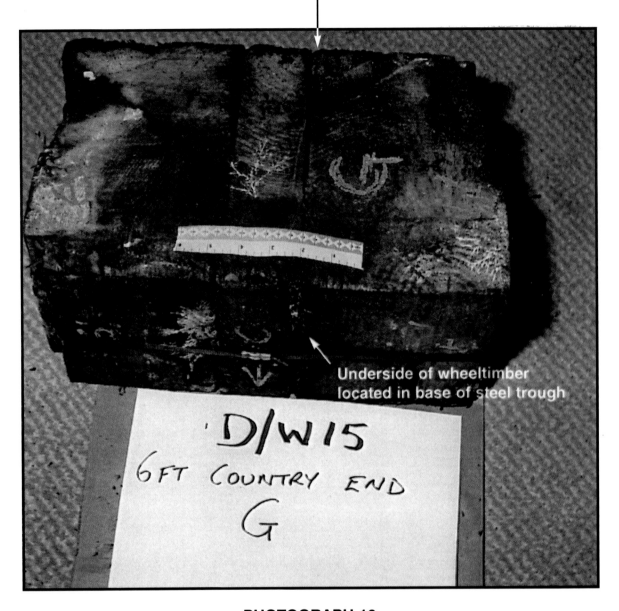

PHOTOGRAPH 10
Cross-section through the six foot wheeltimber at the
Crayford end of Bridge 799.

PHOTOGRAPH 11
The 12th wagon: PR3001 looking back towards Lee showing
the extent of loading with dirty ballast.

List of previous wheeltimber failures recorded on BRR accident database between 01/01/88 to 31/03/98

Date	Location	Vehicle type	BRR investigation
2/11/88	Wanstead Park	Unknown	No
21/5/88	Darlington	PO COV-2 Axle	No
22/7/88	Raynes Park	Locomotive	No
30/11/88	Blackhorse Road, Walthamstow	Bogie Tank 100T+	Yes
6/6/90	Between Wanstead Park and Leytonstone High Road	Bogie Tank 102T	Yes
6/6/90	Darlington	PO Presflo 2AX	Yes
15/3/91	Lostock Hall	Locomotive	No
29/4/92	Rose Grove	Locomotive	No
21/5/92	Between Effingham and Bookham	EMU 319 MS	Yes
6/8/94	Camden Road	2AX Tank 51T	Yes
6/9/94	Barassie	Engineer's Turbot	Yes
13/4/95	Aston between Bescot and Didcot	Coal hopper	Yes
26/7/95	Paddington	Locomotive	Yes
14/11/96	Harrington	DMU 142 DMSL	Yes
4/2/97	Bexley	Bogie box 102T	Yes

APPENDIX 5   List of abbreviations

BRR   British Rail Research
BTP   British transport Police
EWS   English, Welsh and Scottish Railways
HSE   Health and Safety Executive
HSTRC   High Speed Track Recording Coach
HMRI   Her Majesty's Railway Inspectorate
RSC   Railway Safety Case
SEIMCL   South East Infrastructure Maintenance Company Limited
STRCL   Southern Track Renewals Company Limited
TOPS   TOTAL OPERATIONS PROCESSING SYSTEM
TTL   TRADA Technology Limited

APPENDIX 6   Health and Safety Legislation (HSWA)

All the companies involved in this accident are subject to the application of the Health and Safety at Work etc. Act 1974 and various regulations made under this Act, including the Railways (Safety Case) Regulations 1994. HMRI; a part of HSE, is the enforcing authority for health and safety legislation on the national railway network.

Health and Safety at Work etc. Act 1974 (HSWA)

The HSWA seeks to secure the health, safety and welfare of people at work and to protect other people from risks arising from work activities. The Act does this by imposing general duties on employers to ensure that both their employees and others (the public) are protected from the risks arising from the employer's activities.

Railways (Safety Case) Regulations 1994

The Railways (Safety Case) Regulations require railway operators to prepare and secure acceptance of a safety case (RSC) in order to operate. The railway infrastructure controller's RSC must be accepted by HSE. A train operator's RSC must be accepted by the infrastructure controller.

A RSC requires a systematic approach to health and safety. It is a comprehensive working document which describes how a company manages health and safety. It includes the company's resources and structure, details of the risks arising from the company's work and how those risks are controlled, procedures and systems that the company uses to manage these risks and details of the company's monitoring of the effectiveness of these systems. The RSC must be reviewed every three years and this review accepted by the appropriate organisation.

Railways (Safety Critical Work) Regulations 1994

The Railways (Safety Critical Work) Regulations 1994 require employers in the railway industry to ensure that employees carrying out work which is vital to the safe operation of the railway are competent and fit to carry out that work.

These regulations underpin the general duties of an employer to ensure the competence and fitness of their employees for the tasks they undertake. They also provide a mechanism to enable HSE to approve specific assessments and standards to be achieved. The regulations supplement other legal requirements by ensuring that those working on the railway system can be properly identified and their records of competence and fitness checked by HSE inspectors or railway operators.

APPENDIX 7   Maintaining a Safe Railway Infrastructure

In March 1996 the Health and Safety Executive (HSE) published a report; "Maintaining a Safe Railway Infrastructure". This report gives an account of a major in-depth look by HSE between October 1995 and January 1996 at the way in which Railtrack plc sought at that time to secure the continued safety of its railway infrastructure through Railtrack's own management arrangements for the selection, monitoring and control of its infrastructure contractors.

The principal findings were:

We have concluded that the principles of selection and control of infrastructure contractors as set out in Railtrack's Railway Safety Case remain sound but that the formal systems in place to apply these principles need to be improved and greater effort is needed to secure effective operation of systems in practice.

In presenting we must recognise that weaknesses in formal management systems do not necessarily lead directly to accidents, but they can eat away at safety margins and can lead to an increase in risk of harm. In looking at the trends in the occurrence of incidents over recent years we have to conclude that the risks of accidents occurring has not significantly increased. However we do not believe that Railtrack can be confident that such risks will not increase as the nature of the railway industry changes, unless it takes urgent steps to strengthen its systems and the way they are applied. Moreover, HM Railway Inspectorate cannot itself be satisfied that Railtrack's Railway Safety case and relevant statutory provisions are being complied with unless improvements are made. In short there is no room at all for complacency and the findings of this report are highly significant for Railtrack and ourselves as the independent safety regulator.

KEY ACTIONS REQUIRED

The key action points for Railtrack arising out of the report on this exercise are set out below:

Key Action 1. Railtrack should take urgent steps to come fully into compliance with its Railway Safety Case.

Key Action 2. Railtrack should develop its strategy for management of its contractors so as to give coherence to its efforts to monitor and assess contractor performance.

Key Action 3. It is a matter of concern that Railtrack's monitoring of technical performance of its contractors is not yet adequately or effectively developed. As it is Railtrack's policy to continue to use performance contracts it should, as a matter of urgency, ensure that its systems for effective monitoring of the technical performance of its contractors, including their compliance with Railway Group Standards, are made fully effective. Where appropriate, systems should include monitoring and auditing of contractors' self checking procedures.

There were 10 key actions contained in the report.

Railtrack plc should produce, in writing, an improved strategy for monitoring its contractors' performance, and implementation plan for elements within that strategy.

The strategy should cover both monitoring of technical performance, including compliance with all relevant standards, and monitoring of Railtrack's contractors health and safety management systems. Wherever appropriate arrangements for monitoring should be related to the objectives set for contractors.

The strategy should set out clearly the arrangements for monitoring including, in particular:

a)   what monitoring is intended to achieve;

b)   the relationship and interface between various elements of the strategy;

c)   the criteria for deciding the size, timing and nature of programmes for each element of the strategy;

d)   the identification and responsibilities of Railtrack managers who will manage each element of the strategy;

e)   the way in which results of monitoring are to be assessed and recorded; and

f)   who will decide whether remedial action is necessary and what criteria will be used for such judgements.

Printed and published by the Health and Safety Executive
C10   2/99